Go Fly a Kite!

Written by Claire Owen

Japan

My name is Takesh. I live in the city of Kyoto. On windy days, I fly a kite shaped like a hexagon. Have you ever flown a kite? If so, what shape was it? Was it symmetrical? How high did your kite fly? For how long did it stay in the air?

Contents

Wherever you see me, you'll find activities to try and questions to answer.

Japanese Kites

Japan is famous for its colorful kites and for the kite festivals that are held there each year. In Japan, kites are called *tako*, and the picture symbol for the word *kite* is made up of the symbols for *wind* and *cloth*. However, a dictionary from the tenth century shows that kites were first called *kami tobi*, or "paper hawks." Today, Japanese kites come in many shapes and sizes.

Wind

Cloth

Kite

The English word *kite* comes from the name of a bird. In many other languages, the word for *kite* comes from the name of a creature or object that moves like a kite or its string.

Kites Around the World

France	*cerf-volante*	"flying deer"
Germany	*drachen*	"dragon"
Greece	*hartaetos*	"paper eagle"
Italy	*aquilone*	"eagle"
Mexico	*papalote*	"butterfly"
Russia	*zmey*	"snake"
Spain	*cometas*	"comet"

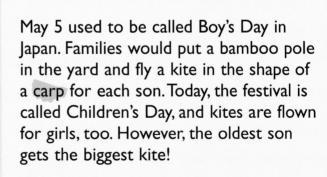

May 5 used to be called Boy's Day in Japan. Families would put a bamboo pole in the yard and fly a kite in the shape of a carp for each son. Today, the festival is called Children's Day, and kites are flown for girls, too. However, the oldest son gets the biggest kite!

carp a freshwater fish with large scales

5

Kite Festivals

Kites play an important part in Japanese culture. Traditionally, kites are flown on New Year's Day, on public holidays, and at festivals. One of Japan's most famous kite festivals is *Hamamatsu*. The festival dates back to the 1500s, when a ruler celebrated the birth of his son by flying a kite decorated with the baby's name. Today, more than two million people watch teams of kite fliers try to bring down each other's kites!

Selected Kite Festivals (2005)

January 1	Ichinomiya New Year Kite Festival
January 3	Tokyo Handmade Kite Festival
January 8–9	Marugame Winter Kite Festival
January 16	Ginowan City Kite Festival
February 11	Nishioji Kite Fly
February 19–20	Kesen-numa Tenbata Matsuri
March 12–13	Goshogawa Kite Fly
March 28	Yokohama Kite Fly
April 2–3	Tadotsu Kite Fly
April 4	Nagasaki Hata Kite Fly
April 29	Itabashi Parents & Children Kite Fly
May 3–5	Hamamatsu Kite Festival
May 21–22	Tahara Kite Festival
June 5–6	Sanjo Giant Kite Fighting Festival
June 25–26	Ishigakijima Kite Festival

Pick two festivals that are in different months. How many days after the end of the first festival is the start of the second festival?

Ancient Kites

The first kites are thought to have been flown in China between 2,500 and 3,000 years ago. Made from bamboo and silk, the earliest kites were probably used in religious ceremonies. People thought that kites could scare away evil spirits or bring good fortune. Kites were probably introduced into Japan from China by Buddhist missionaries around the year 700.

Legend has it that a Chinese farmer got the idea for a kite after the wind blew off his hat and he managed to grab one of the tie-strings.

missionary a person sent out
by a church to
spread its religion
in a foreign
country

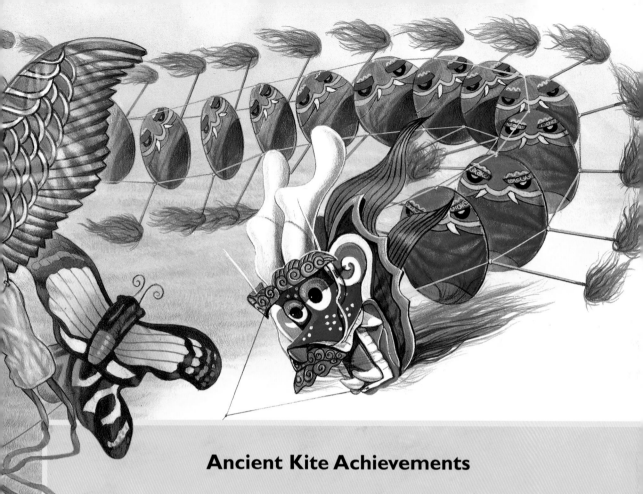

Ancient Kite Achievements

- The Chinese philosopher Mo Zi lived from 478 B.C. to 392 B.C. He spent three years making a wooden flying hawk, only to have it break after a single day's flight!

- In the fifth century B.C., a kite maker named Kungshu P'an made bird-shaped kites that could fly for up to three days.

- In 196 B.C., General Han Hsin and a small band of soldiers dug a tunnel under the walls of an enemy palace. To determine what length to make the tunnel, Han first flew a kite above the palace and then measured the length of its string.

How many years ago did Han Hsin fly his kite? For how many years did Mo Zi live?

B.C.   before Christ; before the year in which Jesus Christ is believed to have been born

Not Just for Fun

Over the centuries, kites have been used in many innovative ways. The Japanese print below shows that builders used kites to help them lift tiles onto the roofs of houses! In Indonesia, fishing lines were suspended from kites made of woven palm leaves. In some places, kites were used to carry fireworks. Kites have also been used in scientific experiments, and they played an important part in the development of the first airplanes.

innovate   to create a new device or a new way of doing something

In 1901, a kite was used to hold a wire in the sky at St. John's in Newfoundland, Canada. This special wire was the experimental aerial that received the first transatlantic radio signal.

Today, kites are the latest piece of equipment for many people who enjoy recreational fishing. Wind-powered kites are used to carry fishing lines up to 980 feet out from shore. By using kites to carry their lines, anglers are able to keep their feet firmly on the beach and still catch large, deep-water fish!

High in the Sky

The most famous scientific experiment that involved
a kite was carried out in America by Benjamin Franklin.
In 1752, Franklin was lucky not to be electrocuted when
he flew a kite during a thunderstorm to investigate the
electrical properties of lightning. At around the same time,
meteorologists were just beginning to use kites to carry
thermometers and other measuring instruments into the
atmosphere.

Franklin's kite was not
struck by lightning, but
static electricity built up
along the string. Franklin
used a silk ribbon to
hold the kite string,
because silk is a poor
conductor of electricity.
However, water is a
good conductor, so
Franklin stood under
cover to keep the
ribbon dry.

meteorologist   a scientist who studies weather, climate,
                 and the atmosphere

Meteorological Milestones

1749   Thermometers carried by kites measure air temperatures at altitudes of up to 3,000 feet.

1840   Kites are used to find the height of rain clouds.

1882   A wind-speed meter is carried by a kite.

1889   Kites are used to investigate cyclones.

1895   A meteograph carried by a kite measures air pressure, temperature, and wind speed.

1898   The United States Weather Bureau opens 17 observation stations that send up instrument-carrying kites at the same time. (The average height of kite observations was 8,700 feet, but in 1907, one flight reached a world-record 23,111 feet.)

1919   The U.S. Weather Bureau discontinues daily measurements with kites.

1933   The last U.S. Weather Bureau kite station closes as airplanes replace kites.

For how many years did the U.S. kite stations make daily observations? Estimate and then calculate the total number of daily observations.

To record the Milestones above, Todd draws a timeline 3 feet long with marks to show 1740, 1750, ... 1940. Could those marks be 2 inches apart?

Flight by Kite

Early stories from Japan and China tell of large kites being used to lift people off the ground. For centuries, this was the closest that humans came to flying. In about 1170, a Japanese warrior named Minamoto was exiled with his son to an island. Minamoto is said to have built a huge kite to carry his son back to the mainland.

exile   to force a person to leave his or her own country
         and live somewhere else

In 1893, an Australian named Lawrence Hargrave invented the box kite. The following year, Hargrave linked four of his kites together, slung a seat below them, and flew a distance of 16 feet. In Massachusetts in 1898, a box kite with about 86 square feet of sail area rose to a height of 12,471 feet.

Hargrave's experiments with box kites influenced other early airplane designers, including the Wright brothers. The picture below, taken in 1906, shows the first airplane flight in Europe.

Use miles and yards to describe how high the box kite flew in 1898. Then find the sail area of the kite to the nearest square yard.

Kite Power

Kites have helped people travel on land, on water, and through the air. When Benjamin Franklin was a boy, he used a kite to pull him along while ice skating. Once, he crossed a mile-wide lake by lying on his back and letting a kite pull him across. In 1826, an English schoolmaster named George Pocock invented a carriage pulled by two kites. In 1903, American Samuel Cody crossed the English Channel in a boat powered by kites.

Pocock's carriage could carry four or five people and travel at speeds up to 20 miles per hour. On one 40-mile journey, Pocock's carriage beat the stagecoach by more than half an hour!

stagecoach   a horse-drawn coach used to carry mail or passengers along a regular route

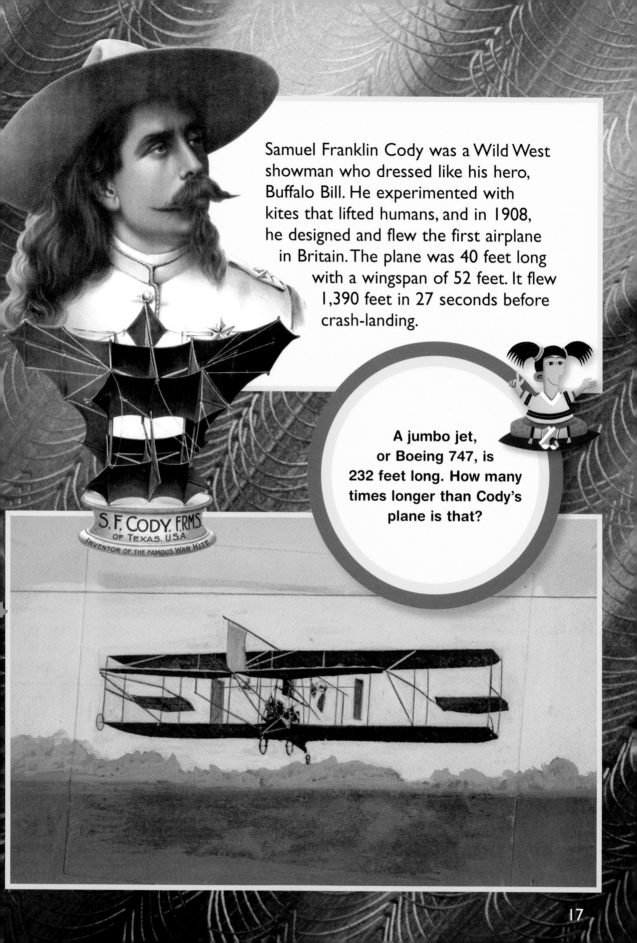

Samuel Franklin Cody was a Wild West showman who dressed like his hero, Buffalo Bill. He experimented with kites that lifted humans, and in 1908, he designed and flew the first airplane in Britain. The plane was 40 feet long with a wingspan of 52 feet. It flew 1,390 feet in 27 seconds before crash-landing.

A jumbo jet, or Boeing 747, is 232 feet long. How many times longer than Cody's plane is that?

S. F. CODY. F.R.M.S.
OF TEXAS. U.S.A.
INVENTOR OF THE FAMOUS WAR KITE

Go Fly a Kite!

Today, kites are used mainly for recreation. Most modern kites are made with lightweight fabric such as ripstop nylon and are easy to fly. They come in a colorful variety of shapes and sizes. Kite flying is an activity that people of all ages and fitness levels can enjoy. More challenging variations of this sport include kite skating, kite skiing, kite surfing, kiteboarding, and kite buggying!

variation   something that is based on something else but is different from it

Kites add speed and power to many traditional sports. Kite-powered sports, known as kite-traction sports, are popular among extreme thrillseekers!

Kite Records

Over the years, many people have set records related to kites. The world's largest kite is the MegaBite, made in 1995 by Peter Lynn of New Zealand. The kite is 210 feet long and 72 feet wide! Laid flat on the ground, the MegaBite's area is 10,042 square feet. The smallest kite, shown below (actual size), measures only $\frac{5}{16}$ inch by $\frac{6}{16}$ inch! It was flown by Shingo Watanabe of Japan in 2001. The world's longest kite, the Cracken, was created in 1990 by Michel Trouillet. It is 3,394 feet long and weighs 233 pounds.

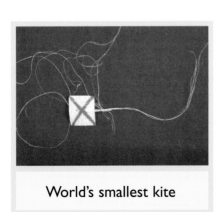

World's smallest kite

World's largest kite, the MegaBite

1. A basketball court is 94 feet long and 50 feet wide. How does the size of the MegaBite compare to the size of a basketball court? (Hint: You could compare the lengths, widths, and areas.)

2. Find and measure a postage stamp. How does it compare in size to the world's smallest kite?

3. About how many times longer than the MegaBite is the Cracken?

4. In 2003, a 192-foot-long train of 230 kites was flown to set a Guinness World Record. On average, how many inches apart were the kites?

Mathematical Kites

In mathematics, a kite is defined as a convex quadrilateral with two pairs of equal adjacent sides. (In a convex shape, all the corners, or vertices, "point" outward, as in Figure *A*.)

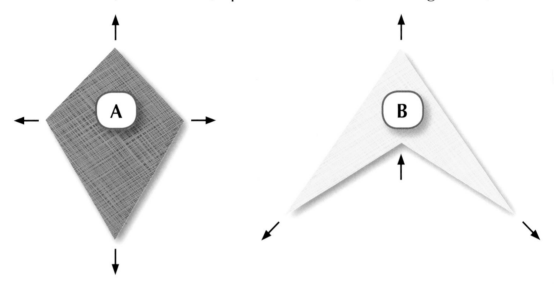

Figure *B* is not a kite. Although it has two pairs of equal adjacent sides, it is not convex. This shape is called a *deltoid*.

The diagonals of any kite are perpendicular, that is, at right angles to each other.

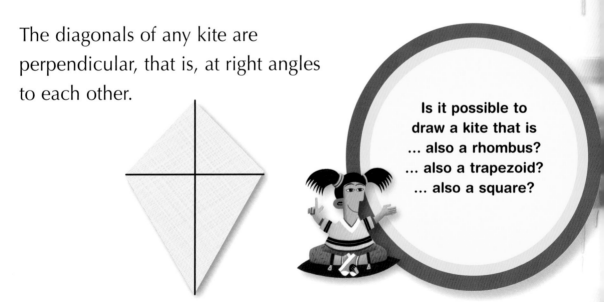

Is it possible to draw a kite that is
... also a rhombus?
... also a trapezoid?
... also a square?

adjacent   next to or adjoining something else

Investigate the Area of a Kite

You will need paper, scissors, tape, a ruler, a pencil, and at least 3 sheets of one-inch grid paper.

1. Cut out a kite of your choice from a sheet of grid paper. Measure the length and the width of your kite (in inches).

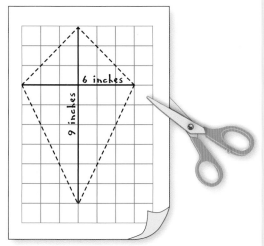

2. Make a chart with the headings *Length*, *Width*, and *Area*. Write the length and width of your kite on the chart.

	Length (inches)	Width (inches)	Area (square inches)
Kite 1	9	6	
Kite 2			
Kite 3			

3. Cut your kite along its diagonals. Arrange the 4 triangles to form a rectangle. Figure out the area of the rectangle and, hence, the kite.

4. Record the area on your chart. Repeat the steps for other paper kites. Can you see a quick way to find the area of a kite?

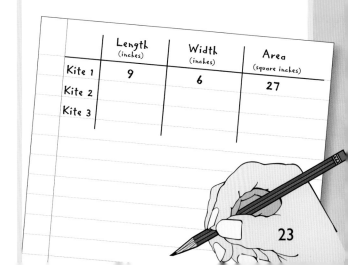

	Length (inches)	Width (inches)	Area (square inches)
Kite 1	9	6	27
Kite 2			
Kite 3			

Sample Answers

Try to find some other kite records, such as the highest a single kite has flown, or the longest time that two kites have been flown at the same time.

Page 9 Mo Zi lived for 86 years.

Page 13 21 years; 7,669, that is, 365 x 21 plus 4 days for leap years (Note: 1900 was not a leap year.)
No (20 x 2 inches = 40 inches)

Page 15 2 miles and 637 yards; 10 square yards

Page 17 5.8 (almost 6) times longer

Page 21 1. length: 116 feet longer; about $2\frac{1}{4}$ times longer
width: 22 feet wider; about $1\frac{1}{2}$ times wider
area: 5,342 square feet bigger; about twice as big
3. about 16 times longer
4. about 10 inches apart

Page 22 yes; no; yes

Index